MACMILLAN/McGRAW

Reading/Language Arts

SKILLS • STRATEGIES

PRACTICE BOOK

FOR COMPREHENSION • VOCABULARY • DECODING AND PHONICS • STUDY SKILLS

MACMILLAN/McGRAW-HILL SCHOOL PUBLISHING COMPANY

New York   Chicago   Columbus

1995 Printing

Macmillan/McGraw-Hill School Division
10 Union Square East
New York, New York 10003

Printed in the United States of America

ISBN 0-02-179169-4 / 1, L.5

7 8 9 BAW 99 98 97

Borders: Dianne Cassidy
Illustrations: Yvette Banek, Kris Cartwright, Cynthia Jabar, Sharon Holm,
John Jones, Deborah Sims, Lynn Sweat, Jill Weber, Bari Weissman

Contents

Comprehension • Vocabulary • Decoding and Phonics • Study Skills

Unit 1: Being Family, Being Friends

HENRY AND MUDGE IN PUDDLE TROUBLE

Make, Confirm, or Revise Predictions
INTERACTIVE READING 1

Summarize   SUM IT UP! 2

Consonant Blends (/spl/*spl*, /squ/*squ*,
/sm/*sm*, /sn/*sn*, /st/*st*)   TURNING BACK
TO LITERATURE 3

Consonant Blends (/spl/*spl*, /squ/*squ*,
/sm/*sm*, /sn/*sn*, /st/*st*) 4

Long Vowels and Phonograms (/ī/-*ight*)
TURNING BACK TO LITERATURE 5

Long Vowels and Phonograms (/ī/-*ight*) 6

Make Inferences   TURNING BACK
TO LITERATURE 7

Make Inferences 8

Diphthongs and Phonograms (/ou/-*own*)
LEARNING THE CODE 9

Diphthongs and Phonograms (/ou/-*own*) 10

EAT UP, GEMMA

Character, Setting, Plot
INTERACTIVE READING 11

Summarize   SUM IT UP! 12

Long Vowels and Phonograms (/ō/-*oke*)
TURNING BACK TO LITERATURE 13

Long Vowels and Phonograms (/ō/-*oke*) 14

Consonant Blends (/fr/*fr*, /gr/*gr*, /br/*br*, /dr/*dr*,
/tr/*tr*)   TURNING BACK TO LITERATURE 15

Consonant Blends (/fr/*fr*, /gr/*gr*, /br/*br*,
/dr/*dr*, /tr/*tr*) 16

Sequence of Events   TURNING BACK
TO LITERATURE 17

Sequence of Events 18

Diphthongs (/oi/-*oy*)   LEARNING THE CODE 19

Diphthongs (/oi/-*oy*) 20

GUINEA PIGS DON'T READ BOOKS

Main Idea and Supporting Details
INTERACTIVE READING 21

Main Idea and Supporting Details;
Summarize   SUM IT UP! 22

Consonant Digraphs (/ch/*ch*, /sh/*sh*, /th/*th*,
/hw/*wh*)   TURNING BACK
TO LITERATURE 23

Consonant Digraphs (/ch/*ch*, /sh/*sh*, /th/*th*,
/hw/*wh*) 24

Diphthongs (/oi/-*oy*)   TURNING BACK
TO LITERATURE 25

Diphthongs (/oi/-*oy*) 26

Diphthongs and Phonograms (/ou/-*ound*)
LEARNING THE CODE 27

Diphthongs and Phonograms (/ou/-*ound*) 28

BABY RATTLESNAKE

Make Inferences; Plot
INTERACTIVE READING 29

Plot; Draw Conclusions; Summarize
SUM IT UP! 30

Inflectional Endings (-*ing*)   TURNING BACK
TO LITERATURE 31

Inflectional Endings (-*ing*) 32

Long Vowels and Phonograms (/ū/-*use*)
TURNING BACK TO LITERATURE **33**
Long Vowels and Phonograms (/ū/-*use*) **34**
Consonant Blends (/sk/*sc*, /sl/*sl*, /sm/*sm*,
/sn/*sn*, /sp/*sp*, /st/*st*) TURNING BACK
TO LITERATURE **35**
Consonant Blends (/sk/*sc*, /sl/*sl*, /sm/*sm*,
/sn/*sn*, /sp/*sp*, /st/*st*) **36**
Make, Confirm, or Revise Predictions
TURNING BACK TO LITERATURE **37**
Make, Confirm, or Revise Predictions **38**
Diphthongs and Phonograms (/ou/-*out*)
TURNING BACK TO LITERATURE **39**
Diphthongs and Phonograms (/ou/-*out*) **40**

INFORMATION ILLUSTRATED

Calendar **41**
Calendar **42**

Unit 2: You're Invited!

FORTUNATELY

Cause and Effect INTERACTIVE READING **43**
Cause and Effect; Summarize SUM IT UP! **44**
Unfamiliar Words TURNING BACK
TO LITERATURE **45**
Unfamiliar Words **46**
Make, Confirm, or Revise Predictions
TURNING BACK TO LITERATURE **47**
Make, Confirm, or Revise Predictions **48**
Diphthongs and Phonograms (/ou/-*ound*)
TURNING BACK TO LITERATURE **49**
Diphthongs and Phonograms (/ou/-*ound*) **50**
Short Vowels and Phonograms (/a/-*an*)
TURNING BACK TO LITERATURE **51**
Short Vowels and Phonograms (/a/-*an*) **52**

Long Vowels and Phonograms (/ē/-*eep*)
LEARNING THE CODE **53**
Long Vowels and Phonograms (/ē/-*eep*) **54**

A BIRTHDAY BASKET FOR TÍA

Spatial Relationships
INTERACTIVE READING **55**
Spatial Relationships; Summarize
SUM IT UP! **56**
Short Vowels and Phonograms (/a/-*at*)
TURNING BACK TO LITERATURE **57**
Short Vowels and Phonograms (/a/-*at*) **58**
Long Vowels and Phonograms (/ē/-*eep*)
TURNING BACK TO LITERATURE **59**
Long Vowels and Phonograms (/ē/-*eep*) **60**
Unfamiliar Words TURNING BACK
TO LITERATURE **61**
Unfamiliar Words **62**
Sequence of Events TURNING BACK
TO LITERATURE **63**
Sequence of Events **64**
Short Vowels and Phonograms (/ī/-*ill*)
LEARNING THE CODE **65**
Short Vowels and Phonograms (/ī/-*ill*) **66**

MR. RABBIT AND THE LOVELY PRESENT

Sequence of Events
INTERACTIVE READING **67**
Sequence of Events; Summarize
SUM IT UP! **68**
Fantasy and Reality TURNING BACK
TO LITERATURE **69**
Fantasy and Reality **70**
Long Vowels and Phonograms (/ī/-*y*)
TURNING BACK TO LITERATURE **71**
Long Vowels and Phonograms (/ī/-*y*) **72**

Unfamiliar Words   TURNING BACK

   TO LITERATURE **73**

Unfamiliar Words **74**

Long Vowels and Phonograms (/ē/-*eed*)

   TURNING BACK TO LITERATURE **75**

Long Vowels and Phonograms (/ē/-*eed*) **76**

Diphthongs (/ou/-*ow*)

   LEARNING THE CODE **77**

Diphthongs (/ou/-*ow*) **78**

A LETTER TO AMY

Character, Setting, Plot

   INTERACTIVE READING **79**

Draw Conclusions; Summarize

   SUM IT UP! **80**

Diphthongs and Phonograms (/ou/-*own*)

   TURNING BACK TO LITERATURE **81**

Diphthongs and Phonograms (/ou/-*own*) **82**

Diphthongs and Phonograms (/ou/-*out*)

   TURNING BACK TO LITERATURE **83**

Diphthongs and Phonograms (/ou/-*out*) **84**

Make, Confirm, or Revise Predictions

   TURNING BACK TO LITERATURE **85**

Make, Confirm, or Revise Predictions **86**

Unfamiliar Words   TURNING BACK

   TO LITERATURE **87**

Unfamiliar Words **88**

Diphthongs and Phonograms (/oi/-*oil*)

   LEARNING THE CODE **89**

Diphthongs and Phonograms (/oi/-*oil*) **90**

INFORMATION ILLUSTRATED

Alphabetical Order **91**

Alphabetical Order **92**

Follow Directions **93**

Follow Directions **94**

Literature Comprehension

Henry and Mudge in Puddle Trouble

To make a prediction, you must think about what may happen in a story. As you read about the story characters, think about what they might do next. Imagine what you might do if you were in the story.

Read each story event in the chart below. Then fill in the chart by making a prediction. Check the story to see if you are right.

What Happened	My Prediction
Henry forgets to ask if he can play outside.	
Henry and Mudge see a giant puddle.	
Henry's father cannot find Henry or Mudge.	
Henry's father finds Henry in the puddle.	

Literature Comprehension

Henry and Mudge in Puddle Trouble

Can you guess what might happen when Henry, his father, and Mudge go home?

Write what you think Henry might say to his mother. Use what you have written to summarize the story.

 "Henry, why did you and Mudge go out?"

 " _____

_____ "

 "Where did you get so wet?"

 " _____

_____ "

 "What did Dad do right after he found you?"

 " _____

_____ "

 "How did Dad get so wet?"

 " _____

_____ "

Macmillan/McGraw-Hill

Make Inferences

Henry and Mudge in Puddle Trouble

How do you think Henry's dad feels when he yells, "Henry!"? People often yell when they are not happy. So you can infer that Henry's dad is probably upset.

Follow these directions. Make inferences using what you read and what you already know.

1. Reread page 16. Why was Henry getting bored?

   _____

   _____

2. Reread page 19. How do you think Henry felt when he saw the giant puddle?

   _____

   _____

3. Reread page 27. Why do you think Henry yelled, "Mudge!"?

   _____

   _____

Macmillan/McGraw-Hill

Make Inferences

To make an inference, think about what you have read as well as what you already know.

Read each story. Make inferences to answer each question. Then circle the letter next to your answer.

1. It was summer. Jane jumped into the pool. She began to feel better.

How had Jane felt before she jumped in?
a. tired
b. sad
c. hot

2. Scott did not make his bed. He did not put away his toys. He did not hang up his coat.

How was Scott acting?
a. careless
b. happy
c. helpful

3. Clara ate breakfast. Then she ran out of the house with her books. She waited for the bus.

Where was Clara going?
a. to a party
b. to school
c. to grandma's house

4. Nate walked to the park. He had his bat and glove. He met his friends. They picked teams.

What was Nate going to do?
a. ride his bike
b. read a book
c. play baseball

4

Diphthong *own*

...ell d**own** in the puddle.

Read each sentence. Use the words in the box to finish each sentence.

clown	frown	brown	crown	tow..	down

1. Henry began to_____ .

2. Rain was falling_____ .

3. Henry did not want to go to_____ .

4. He did not want to dress up like a _____ .

5. He did not want to put on a gold _____ .

6. He did want to play in the _____ mud!

Diphthong *own*

clown

Say each picture name. Listen to the beginning sound or sounds. Write the letter or letters that complete each word.

1.

t   d

___**own**

2.

cl   cr

___**own**

3.

fr   br

___**own**

4.

d   dr

___**own**

5.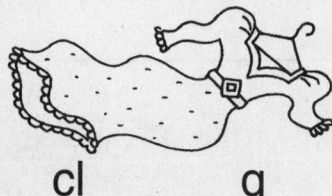

cl   g

___**own**

6.

br   cr

___**own**

Macmillan/McGraw-Hill

EAT UP, GEMMA

Thinking about story characters and what they do to solve a problem can help you understand what you read.

Read or reread "Eat Up, Gemma." Think of what each character did to help Gemma. Then fill in the chart. Use the chart to retell the story.

Who tried to help Gemma?	What did they give Gemma?
Mom	
man at the fruit stand	
Grandma	
Dad	
Gemma's brother	

5

Level 5   EAT UP, GEMMA

Interactive Reading
ANALYZE STORY ELEMENTS: Character, Setting, Plot

Literature Comprehension

EAT UP, GEMMA

Sometimes people keep baby books. They write about important things in a baby's life. Imagine that this page is part of Gemma's baby book. Write the important things that happened when she wouldn't eat.

When Gemma was little, she had a problem.

_____

_____.

Everyone said, "_____

_____." They gave her

_____

_____.

Gemma's problem was solved when _____

_____

_____.

Macmillan/McGraw-Hill

Phonogram *oke*

EAT UP, GEMMA

Gemma w**oke** up late.

Read each sentence. Circle the word that completes the sentence. Then write the word on the line.

broke

1. The boy gave Gemma a little _____. **spoke**

poke

_____

joke

2. Gemma laughed at the _____. **smoke**

broke

_____

stroke

3. Dad listened, and then he _____. **spoke**

joke

_____

joke

4. Eat slowly or you might _____. **poke**

choke

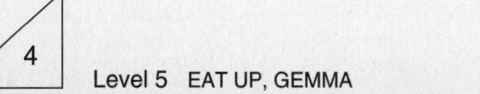
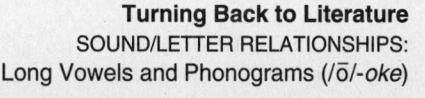

Phonogram *oke*

What a funny j**oke**!

Read each clue. Then use the words from the word box to solve this puzzle.

poke	smoke	stroke	joke	spoke	choke

Down

1. It can happen when eating.

2. A fire makes this.

5. This is a little jab.

Across

3. A cat likes this.

4. Another word for talked.

6. It makes you laugh.

8

EAT UP, GEMMA

Gemma **drinks** a **breakfast treat.**

She likes **fr**uit juice and **gr**apes.

Name the pictures. Then read the words. Circle the word with the same beginning sounds.

1.

gray   tray

2.

fright   bright

3.

dry   try

4.

tap   trap

5.

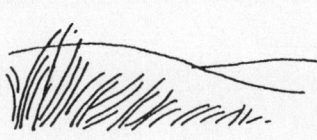

drab   grab

6.

brave   grave

7.

brag   drag

8.

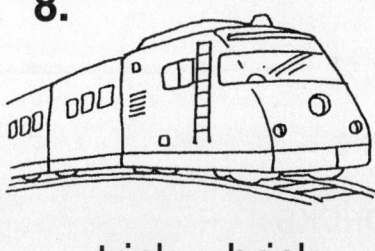

trick   brick

9.

bray   fry

Consonant Blends *fr, gr, br, dr, tr*

 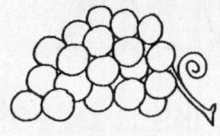 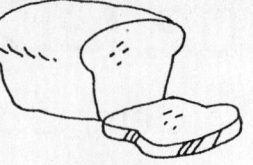  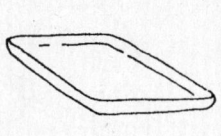

frog   **grapes**   **bread**   **dress**   **tray**

Look at each picture. Then read the question. Underline the word that answers the question. Then write the word.

Is it a picture of

1.

some grass
or some brass? _____

2.

someone frying
or drying? _____

3.

a frown
or a gown? _____

4.

a trip
or a drip? _____

5.

some bricks
or some tricks? _____

EAT UP, GEMMA

The order in which things happen is called the sequence of events. Thinking about the sequence of events can help you understand the story better.

The pictures in each row show something that happened in "Eat Up, Gemma." Number each row of pictures from 1 to 3 to show the order in which things happened.

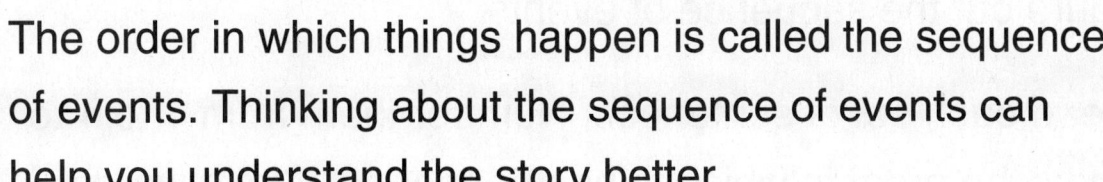

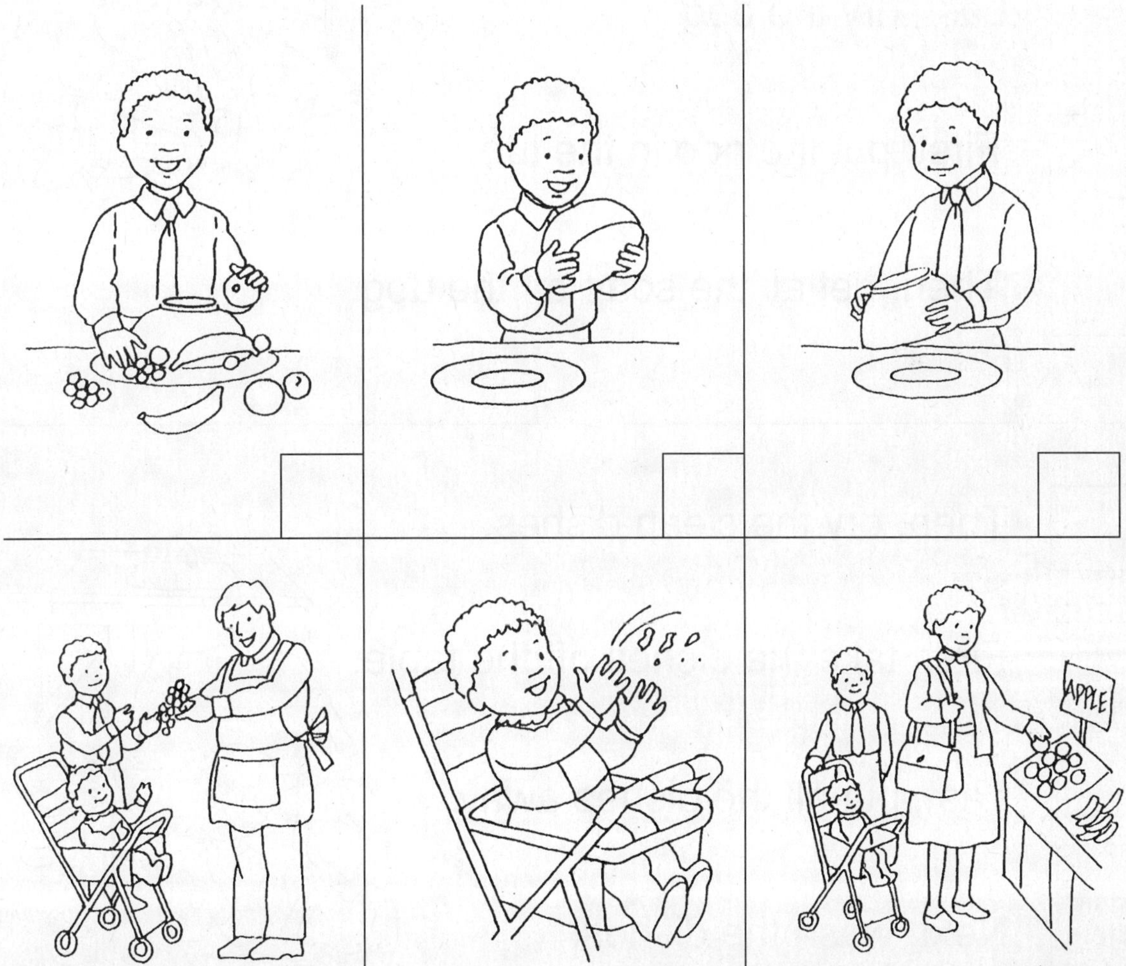

Macmillan/McGraw-Hill

Sequence of Events

Words such as **first**, **next**, **then**, and **last** can help you figure out the sequence of events.

Read each set of sentences. Number them from 1 to 4 to show the order in which things happened. Circle words that helped you figure out the sequence.

□ Next, wash the dog with soap.

□ Last, dry the dog.

□ First, put the dog in the tub.

□ Then, get all the soap off the dog.

□ Then, dry the clean dishes.

□ First, take the dishes off the table.

□ Last, put all the dishes away.

□ Next, wash the dishes.

Macmillan/McGraw-Hill

8

Diphthong *oy*

Gemma will ann**oy** Mom.

Read each sentence. Circle the word that completes the sentence. Then write the word on the line.

1.

Gemma does not _____ eating.

joy   enjoy   annoy

_____

2.

Gemma sleeps with a _____ .

joy   toy   coy

_____

3.

Gemma likes the boy's _____ hat.

coy   joy   cowboy

_____

4.

Everyone feels _____ when Gemma eats.

toy   boy   joy

Diphthong *oy*

cowboy

Say each picture name. Circle and write the word that names the picture.

1.

   boy

   toy   _____

   coy

2.

   annoy

   enjoy   _____

   coy

3.

   cowboy

   newsboy _____

   batboy

4.

   coy

   joy   _____

   toy

5.

   boy

   soy   _____

   might

5

Guinea Pigs Don't Read Books

A main idea is a big idea that the author wants to share. To help explain this big idea, an author uses details or examples.

Read or reread "Guinea Pigs Don't Read Books." List two details that tell more about each main idea.

Guinea pigs have sharp senses.

1. _____

2. _____

Guinea pigs make sounds.

1. _____

2. _____

Guinea pigs have different kinds of fur coats.

1. _____

2. _____

Guinea Pigs Don't Read Books

Imagine that you have entered a guinea pig in a pet show. Fill out this form telling about your pet. Write your answers to each question.

1. What kind of pet are you entering in the show?

_____

_____

2. What does your pet look like?

_____

_____

3. What does your pet eat?

_____

_____

4. What makes your pet a good pet friend?

_____

_____

Guinea Pigs Don't Read Books

When **Sh**el is at school, his guinea pig loves to **ch**ew **th**ings.

Look at each picture. Then circle the letters that stand for the sound you hear at the beginning of the picture name.

1.

ch   sh

2.

wh   th

3.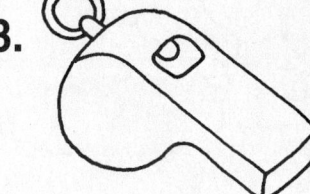

wh   ch

4.

th   sh

5.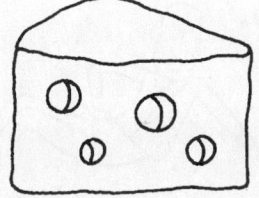

ch   sh

6.

wh   sh

7.

wh   th

8.

sh   ch

9.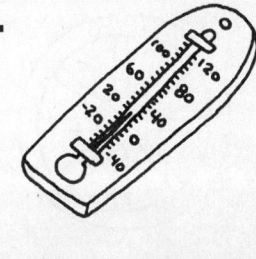

th   sh

9

Level 5   GUINEA PIGS DON'T READ BOOKS

Turning Back to Literature
SOUND/LETTER RELATIONSHIPS:
Consonant Digraphs (/ch/*ch*, /sh/*sh*, /th/*th*, /wh/*wh*)

Consonant Digraphs ch, sh, th, wh

cherry

shark

thirteen

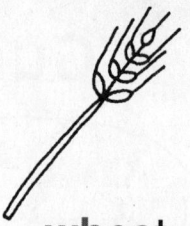
wheat

Look at each picture. Write **ch, sh, th,** or **wh** to finish each picture name.

1.
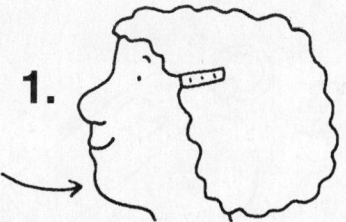
____ **in**

2.

____ **ite**

3.

____ **umb**

4.
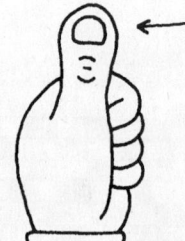
____ **ip**

5.

____ **in**

6.

____ **ild**

7.

____ **eel**

8.

____ **ave**

9.

____ **ale**

24 SOUND/LETTER RELATIONSHIPS:
Consonant Digraphs (/ch/*ch*, /sh/*sh*, /th/*th*, /wh/*wh*)   Level 5   GUINEA PIGS DON'T READ BOOKS

9

Guinea Pigs Don't Read Books

enj**oy**   ann**oy**

Usually people enjoy their pets. But sometimes a pet can be annoying! Look at each picture. Do you think the word **enjoy** or **annoy** describes the person? Circle the word that tells about each picture.

1.

enjoy   annoy

2.

enjoy   annoy

3.

enjoy   annoy

4.

enjoy   annoy

Diphthong *oy*

Ro**y** and **Tr**o**y** are b**oy**s.

Say each picture name. Write the word that tells about each picture.

1.

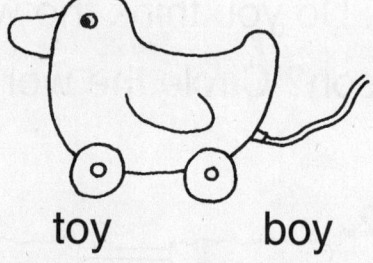

toy   boy

_____

2.

annoy   joy

_____

3.

boy   joy

_____

4.

enjoy   annoy

_____

5.

enjoy   annoy

_____

6.

batboy   cowboy

_____

Diphthong *ound*

A guinea pig weighs about a **pound**.

Read each sentence. Circle the word that completes the sentence. Then write the word on the line.

1.

Does your _____ like guinea pigs?

round   bound   hound

2.

We finally _____ our guinea pig.

found   ground   sound

3.

Guinea pigs make a squeaking _____.

mound   sound   pound

4.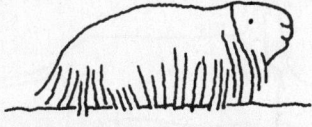

Its long coat touches the _____.

bound   round   ground

Diphthong *ound*

round

Read the words in the box. Then write the word that tells about each picture.

sound	hound	mound	pound	found	ground

1.

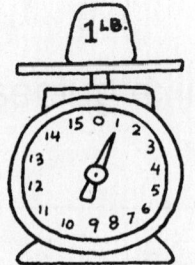

_____

2.

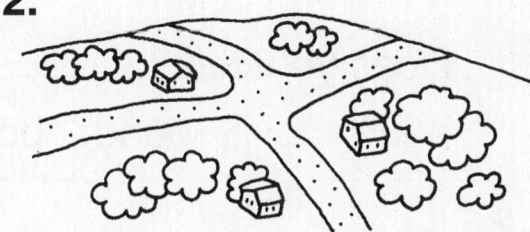

_____

3.

_____

4.

_____

5.

_____

6.

_____

Macmillan/McGraw-Hill

Literature Comprehension

Baby Rattlesnake

Often a reader can infer or guess how a character feels by looking at story pictures.

Read or reread "Baby Rattlesnake." Then look at the pictures below. Finish the sentences to tell how Baby Rattlesnake feels in each picture. Then use the pictures to help you retell the story.

1.

He feels _____.

2.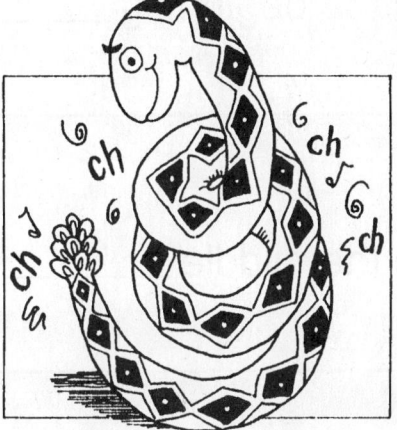

He feels _____.

3.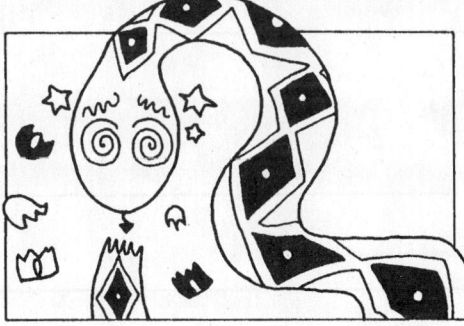

He feels _____.

4.

He feels _____.

Macmillan/McGraw-Hill

4

Level 5   BABY RATTLESNAKE

Interactive Reading
MAKE INFERENCES/
ANALYZE STORY ELEMENTS: Plot   **29**

Baby Rattlesnake

Can you be a storyteller like Te Ata? You can if you remember what happens in the story. Write the important ideas for each part of the story. Then use what you wrote to tell "Baby Rattlesnake" to a friend.

In the beginning _____

_____

In the middle _____

_____

In the end _____

_____

Baby Rattlesnake learned that _____

_____

_____

Macmillan/McGraw-Hill

Baby Rattlesnake

These rules can help you add **ing** to a base word.

- If the base word ends in **e**, drop the **e** and add **ing.**   hid**e** + **ing** = **hiding**

- If the base word ends with a single consonant, double the consonant and add **ing.**   si**t** + **ing** = **sitting**

- For other words, add **ing** to the base word.   cry + **ing** = **crying**

Add the **ing** ending to each word below. Write the new word in the correct column of the chart.

wipe	**step**	**cry**	**act**	**rattle**
dance	**hop**	**love**	**come**	**run**
go	**have**	**rub**	**crush**	**get**

Drop the **e** and add **ing**.	Double the consonant and add **ing**.	Just add **ing**.

Macmillan/McGraw-Hill

Inflectional Ending *ing*

wishing = wish + **ing**   **hoping** = hope **+ ing**

clapping = clap + **ing**

Read each sentence. Circle the word in which **ing** has been added to a base word. Then write the base word.

1. Mr. Lui is talking to Jon. _____

2. Anne is wrapping a gift. _____

3. The cat is napping. _____

4. Mr. Diaz is wiping the dishes. _____

5. Who was baking a cake? _____

6. The baby was sleeping. _____

7. Is Bing using the hose? _____

8. Rick is playing the guitar. _____

Macmillan/McGraw-Hill

Baby Rattlesnake

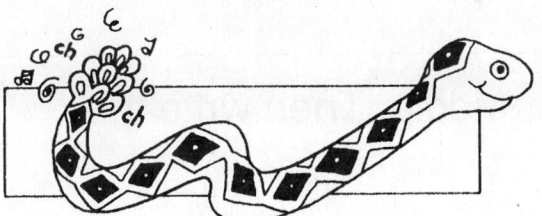 Baby Rattlesnake did not **use** his rattle carefully.

Choose a word in the box to complete each sentence. Then write the word in the sentence.

| amuse | excuse | confused | refused |

1. At first, Mother and Father _____ to give Baby Rattlesnake a rattle.

2. Baby Rattlesnake did not _____ the Rattlesnake People when he cried all night.

3. Baby Rattlesnake was _____ about how to use his rattle.

4. The chief's daughter did not _____ Baby Rattlesnake for scaring her.

Phonogram *use*

Use a f**use**.

Circle the word that answers the riddle. Then write the word.

1. You do this when you use something again.

   _____

   confuse

   amuse

   reuse

2. You feel this way when something makes you laugh.

   _____

   amused

   excused

   confused

3. You do this when you say no.

   _____

   reuse

   refuse

   fuse

4. You feel this way when you are mixed-up.

   _____

   confused

   reused

   amused

Consonant Blends sc, sl, sm, sn, sp, st

Baby Rattlesnake

   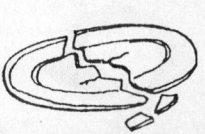

snake   scarf   sled   spider   stamp   smash

Say each picture name. Circle the letters that stand for the beginning sounds.

1.  sl st	**2.**  sc sm	**3.**  sn sm
4.  st sl	**5.**  sl sc	**6.** 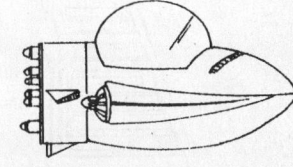 sp st
7.  sl st	**8.**  sm sn	**9.**  sm sp

Macmillan/McGraw-Hill

Consonant Blends *sc, sl, sm, sn, sp, st*

| scout | slide | smell | snail | speed | stop |

Say each picture name. Circle the words that have the same beginning sounds.

1.    speed   snake   snub   slit

2. 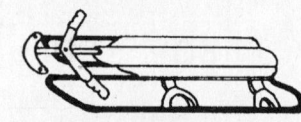   sleet   snip   sped   slip

3. 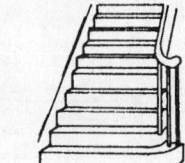   smug   stake   spade   step

4.    sly   scold   scuff   spy

5.    spin   stay   snow   spoke

6.    snub   smoke   slug   smog

12

Baby Rattlesnake

When you read, ask yourself what will happen next. Then read on to see if your prediction is correct. This can help you better understand a story.

Read each story event below. Then fill in the chart by making a prediction of what will happen. Check the story to see if your prediction is correct.

Story Event	My Prediction
Baby Rattlesnake cries all night because he does not have a rattle.	
An elder says Baby Rattlesnake will get in trouble with his rattle.	
Baby Rattlesnake does not listen to warnings about his rattle.	
Baby Rattlesnake darts at the chief's daughter.	

Make, Confirm, or Revise Predictions

Clues in a story can help you make a prediction. Read each story. Then answer each question. Fill in the circle by the answer. Then underline the clues in the story that helped you predict.

1. Jack's friends hid. Jack's mom turned off the light. Then Jack walked into the dark house with his dad.

   What will Jack's friends do?
   ○ stay behind the sofa
   ○ shout "Surprise!"
   ○ leave the house

2. Lunch was over. Mrs. Wright asked the children to get floor mats. They then sat on the floor by the piano.

   What will the children do next?
   ○ eat lunch
   ○ take a test
   ○ sing a song

3. Beth got her pail and shovel. Marie got her float. Mom put towels in a bag.

   Where are they going?
   ○ to the ballgame
   ○ to the lake
   ○ to the circus

4. Phil's dog was very hungry. She watched Phil put the cake on the table. Then Phil left the room.

   What will the dog do?
   ○ fall asleep
   ○ sit up and beg
   ○ eat the cake

Macmillan/McGraw-Hill

8

Baby Rattlesnake

The chief's daughter gave
a sh**out**!

Look at the pictures. Read the words. Then write the
two words that tell about the picture.

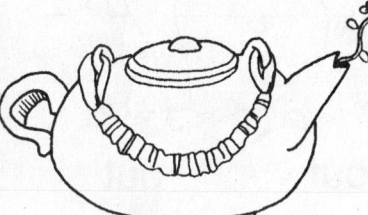

| sprout | spot |
| shout | spout |

1. The _____ is in the _____ .

| snout | trout |
| scout | trot |

2. The _____ fishes for _____ .

| shout | bout |
| spout | pout |

3. The _____ made him _____ .

Macmillan/McGraw-Hill

| 6 |

Level 5   BABY RATTLESNAKE

Phonogram *out*

trout

Say each picture name. Read the words. Write the word that belongs with each picture.

1.

shout   sprout

_____

2.

about   out

_____

3.

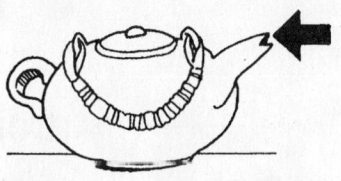

sprout   spout

_____

4.

shout   snout

_____

5.

snout   trout

_____

6.

spout   scout

_____

Name **Olivia** _____ Date _____

Baby Rattlesnake

A calendar is a chart showing the days, weeks, and months of the year.

Use the calendar on page 272 of your book. Answer these questions.

MARCH

S	M	T	W	T	F	S
		1	2	3	4	5	6
7	8	9	10	11	12	13
14	15	16	17	18	19	20
21	22	23	24	25	26	27
28	29	30	31			

JANUARY

SUN	MON	TUE	WED	THU	FRI	SAT
		1	2	3	4	5
6	7	8	9	10	11	12
13	14	15	16	17	18	19
20	21	22	23	24	25	26
27	28	29	30	31		

1. How many months are in a year? **12**

2. What is the first month of the year? **January**

3. What is the shortest month? **Febuary**

4. What month comes right after September? **Octuber**

5. How many days are in a week? **7**

6. On what date were you born? **Jan, 28th 2003**

7. What month of the year do you like best? **January**

8. What day of the week do you like best? **Seterday**

Calendar

Many calendars show each month on a separate page. Use this calendar to answer the questions below.

J u n e						
SUN	MON	TUE	WED	THUR	FRI	SAT
		1	2	3	4	5
6	7	8	9	10	11	12
13	14 Flag Day	15	16	17	18	19
20	21	22	23	24	25	26
27	28	29	30			

1. What month is this calendar for?

    June

2. What day of the week is June 21?

    monday

3. What is the last day of the month?

    _30_

4. What holiday is celebrated on June 14?

    Flag Day

5. What is the date of the third Thursday of June on this calendar?

    June third 2010

6. How many Saturdays are there in the month?

    _4_

Literature Comprehension

Fortunately

Often one event in a story causes another event to happen. In some stories, causes and their effects make up a pattern.

Read or reread "Fortunately." Then look at the chart. Write what happens after each event. Look for a pattern in the chart. Talk about the pattern with a partner.

Ned wants to go to a party in Florida. →	
The airplane motor explodes. →	
The parachute has a hole in it. →	
There is a pitchfork in the haystack. →	
Ned misses the haystack. →	

Fortunately

What things happened to Ned on his way to the party?
Look at each picture. Circle the sentence that tells why it
happened.

1.

The airplane exploded.

The airplane was crowded.

2.

Ned forgot his parachute.

Ned missed the haystack.

3.

Ned wanted to plant flowers.

Tigers were chasing after Ned.

4.

Sharks were swimming after Ned.

Ned was very hot.

Fortunately

Sometimes the other words in a sentence can help you figure out the meaning of an unfamiliar word.

Read each sentence. Use other words in the sentence to help you figure out the meaning of the underlined word. Fill in the circle next to the meaning.

1. Unfortunately the motor **exploded** with a bang.
    - ○ ran very quietly
    - ○ blew up suddenly
    - ○ started without a problem

2. Fortunately Ned had a **parachute** to put on.
    - ○ something people use to jump safely from an airplane
    - ○ a seat found on an airplane
    - ○ part of a motor that can explode

3. Fortunately there was a **haystack** on the ground.
    - ○ machine used on a farm
    - ○ tall smokestack on a building
    - ○ a large pile of hay on the ground

Unfamiliar Words

When you see a word you do not know, think about the other words in the sentence. Often these words can help you figure out the meaning of an unfamiliar word.

Use the words in the following sentences to figure out the meaning of the underlined word. Circle the meaning.

1. Cindy rides down a snowy hill on her **toboggan**.
   A toboggan is:

   a kind of skate   a kind of sled

             a kind of boot

2. Bill picked some red roses and purple **violets**.
   Violets are:

   a kind of flower   a kind of apple

             a kind of bean

3. The **falcon** flew from tree to tree.
   A falcon is:

   a type of airplane   a type of car

             a type of bird

4. Mr. Marks washed his clothes at the **laundromat**.
   A laundromat is:

   a place to buy clothes   a place to eat

             a place to wash clothes

Macmillan/McGraw-Hill

Fortunately

Some stories like "Fortunately" follow a pattern. Finding the pattern makes it easier to predict what will happen.

Read each story event in the chart. Then fill in the chart by predicting what happens next. Check the story to see if your predictions are correct.

Story Event	My Prediction
The airplane motor explodes.	
The parachute has a hole in it.	
The boy is about to land on a haystack.	
The boy misses the haystack.	
The boy lands in the water.	

Make, Confirm, or Revise Predictions

As you read, story clues and what you know can help you make predictions. Read each story. Then fill in the circle next to the event you predict will happen next.

1. Deb fills a big tub with water. She asks her mom for some soap. Then she calls the dog.

What will Deb do next?
- ○ wash her hair
- ◉ wash the dog
- ○ water the flowers

2. Tom fills a bag with dry bread. He goes to the park and sits on a bench.

What will Tom do next?
- ◉ feed the birds
- ○ feed the tigers
- ○ feed the sharks

3. Mrs. Pine tells the children to get their coats. She takes some big balls from the closet.

What will the children do next?
- ○ get on the bus
- ◉ go outside to play
- ○ put on a play

4. Kate has a small shovel and some dirt. Mario has little packs filled with seeds.

What will the children do next?
- ○ pick some flowers
- ○ cut the grass
- ◉ plant a garden

Phonogram *ound*

Fortunately

Ned was **bound** for a party in Florida.

Read each sentence. Circle the word that completes each sentence. Then write the word.

mound
(sound)
wound

1. When the motor exploded, it made a loud __sound__.

(found)
hound
ground

2. Ned __found__ himself falling through the air.

hound
bound
(mound)

3. He saw a big __Mound__ of hay.

(ground)
sound
round

4. He missed the hay and almost hit the __ground__!

(pound)
mound
wound

5. He __pound__ up in water with a lot of sharks.

one p**ound**

Read each riddle. Then read the words at the bottom of the page. Write the word that answers each riddle.

1. This is the shape of a ball. _____

2. You can do this with a hammer. _____

3. A dog is sometimes called this. _____

4. It means to get something back that was lost. _____

5. A pile is sometimes called this. _____

6. Something you hear is called this. _____

| **hound** | **mound** | **round** | **sound** | **found** | **pound** |

Macmillan/McGraw-Hill

Phonogram *an*

Fortunately

Ned **ran** from the tigers.

Look at each picture. Then read the question. Underline the word that answers the question. Then write the word. Is the picture:

1. a van or a span? _____

2. a pan or a man? _____

3. a fan or a tan? _____

4. a clan or a plan? _____

5. a can or a pan? _____

6. bran or a plan? _____

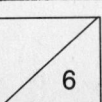

6

Phonogram *an*

Fran r**an**.

Read each clue. Then change the first letter of the word **ran** to make a new word that belongs with the clue.

1. use this to cook   _____

2. use this when it is hot   _____

3. food is stored in this   _____

4. use this to go places   _____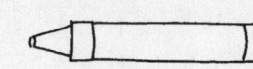

5. a color of a crayon   _____

6. a boy becomes this   _____

Macmillan/McGraw-Hill

Phonogram *eep*

Ned swam in **deep** water.

Say each picture name. Listen to the beginning sound or sounds. Write the letter or letters that complete each word.

1.

(j)   p

___j___ **eep**

2.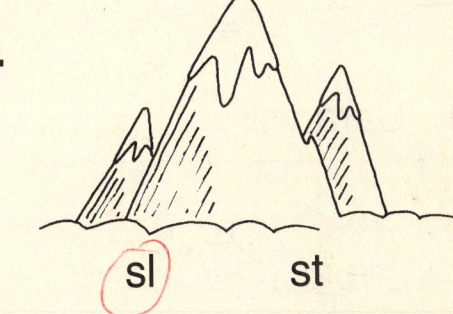

(sl)   st

___sl___ **eep**

3.

st   (sh)

___sh___ **eep**

4.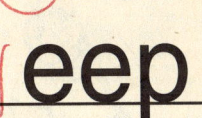

p   (w)

___w___ **eep**

5.

(sw)   st

___sw___ **eep**

6.

(sl)   sh

___sl___ **eep**

Macmillan/McGraw-Hill

6

Level 5 FORTUNATELY

Learning the Code
SOUND/LETTER RELATIONSHIPS: Phonograms (/ē/-*eep*)   **53**

Phonogram *eep*

steep

Circle and write the word that completes each sentence.

1. Sara will _____ the horn.

beep
sweep
deep

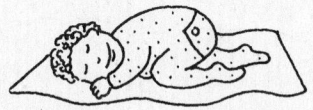

2. The baby likes to _____ .

sleep
steep
seep

3. Look at the _____ .

deep
beep
jeep

4. Roy will _____ up the mess.

sweep
sleep
steep

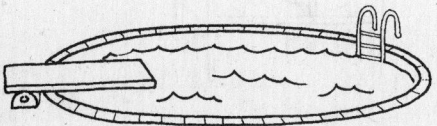

5. The pool is very _____ .

weep
keep
deep

A Birthday Basket for Tía

Remembering sizes, shapes, and where things are can help you understand and remember what you read.

Read or reread "A Birthday Basket for Tía." Then draw in order the things Cecilia put in the basket.

When you are done, you will have **six** things in the basket. Then use your basket as a story map to retell the story to a partner.

A Birthday Basket for Tía

Look at the drawing you made of the birthday basket.
Use it to write a summary of "A Birthday Basket for Tía."

Write your summary as a thank-you note from Aunt Tía
to Cecilia. Tell things in the order Cecilia put them into
the basket.

Dear Cecilia,

Thank you for my birthday basket. I loved getting

1. _____

2. _____

3. _____

4. _____

5. _____

6. _____

Love, Aunt Tía

A Birthday Basket for Tía

Chica is a cat.

Circle the word that answers the riddle.

Then write the word.

1. It goes on a head.

fat   hat   bat

_____

2. It is a little rug.

mat   sat   vat

_____

3. It does not like cats.

pat   mat   rat

_____

4. Use it to hit a ball.

fat   bat   hat

_____

Phonogram *at*

sat

Read the words below. Then write the word that names each picture.

| cat | flat | rat | hat | mat | bat |

1.

_____

2.

_____

3.

_____

4.

_____

5.

_____

6.

_____

Macmillan/McGraw-Hill

A Birthday Basket for Tía

"Can you **keep** a secret?" asked Cecilia.

Read the words in the box below. Underline the three letters that are the same in each word.

creep	**keep**	**jeep**

Build new words by choosing a letter to write on each line.

a   b   d   e   f   i   p   w   x   st   ch

1. _____ **eep**   2. _____ **eep**

3. _____ **eep**   4. _____ **eep**

5. _____ **eep**   6. _____ **eep**

Macmillan/McGraw-Hill

Phonogram *eep*

 sh**eep**

Say each picture name. Circle and write the word that names the picture.

1.

beep
jeep
deep

_____

2.

sweep
sheep
sleep

_____

3.

weep
beep
creep

_____

4.

seep
sweep
steep

_____

Macmillan/McGraw-Hill

Unfamiliar Words

A Birthday Basket for Tía

Things in a group are often alike in some important way.

Use the words in each sentence to help you figure out the underlined word. Circle the picture that goes with the underlined word.

1. Mamá is cutting fruit — pineapple, watermelon, and <u>mangoes</u>.

2. The musicians begin to play their instruments — <u>guitars</u>, violins, drums, and horns.

3. Mamá and Cecilia fill the living room with decorations — balloons, flowers, and a <u>piñata</u>.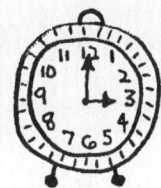

4. Cecilia looks through all her favorite toys — her little pots, her piggy bank, her tin fish, and her <u>dancing puppet</u>.

Unfamiliar Words

Sometimes words in a list can help you figure out a word you do not know.

Read each list of words. Circle any words you do not know. Then use the words you do know in each list to help you figure out the words you circled. Write what each list names. Use the words at the bottom of the page.

1. doll, kite, tricycle _____

2. cat, pig, antelope _____

3. beans, meat, potatoes _____

4. bedroom, living room, kitchen _____

5. car, bus, tractor _____

6. pants, dress, jacket _____

machines   clothing   rooms   foods   animals   toys

Macmillan/McGraw-Hill

A Birthday Basket for Tía

Knowing the sequence of events can help you make sense of what is happening in a story.

Read or reread page 191. Find out the order in which Cecilia and Mamá did things. Now read the sentences below. Write the numbers 1, 2, 3, 4 to show the order in which things happen.

☐ Next Mamá and Cecilia fill the living room with balloons.

☐ Last Cecilia helps Mamá set the table with tiny cakes.

☐ First Mamá and Cecilia fill a piñata with candy.

☐ Then Cecilia helps Mamá set the table with flowers.

Macmillan/McGraw-Hill

Sequence of Events

Sometimes we do things in a special order.

    First put on your socks.

    Next put on your shoes.

    Last tie your shoes.

Read each group of sentences. Then put them in order.
Write the numbers 1, 2, 3, or 4 in each box.

☐   Then cover up the seed with dirt.

☐   First dig a hole in the dirt.

☐   Next drop in a seed.

☐   Last water the dirt.

☐   Next put the bread in the toaster.

☐   Last put jam on the toast.

☐   Then turn on the toaster.

☐   First get out some bread.

8

Macmillan/McGraw-Hill

Mr. Rabbit and the Lovely Present

Thinking about the order in which things happen can help you remember a story.

Read or reread "Mr. Rabbit and the Lovely Present." Use crayons to color the paint jars to match the colors in the story. Under each jar, list 3 gift ideas for that color.

   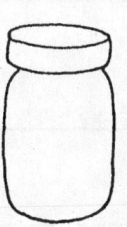

_____   _____

_____   _____

_____   _____

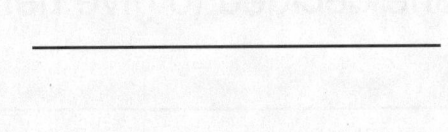

_____   _____

_____   _____

_____   _____

Macmillan/McGraw-Hill

Mr. Rabbit and the Lovely Present

Imagine you are Mr. Rabbit. Sum up what happened when you met the little girl.

Today I met _____

_____ . She told me

_____

_____

_____

Next I gave her a lot of ideas. She decided to give her

mother _____ ,

_____ ,

_____ , and _____ .

Finally the little girl _____

_____

_____

_____ .

Macmillan/McGraw-Hill

Mr. Rabbit and the Lovely Present

Sometimes characters and events in a story are not real. Thinking about things that are real and things that are make-believe can help you understand a story.

Which of these things in "Mr. Rabbit and the Lovely Present" are make-believe? Which are things that could be real? Circle your answer.

1. A rabbit talks to a little girl.   Real
                                                              Make-Believe

2. A rabbit holds a little girl's hand.   Real
                                                              Make-Believe

3. A canary sits in a tree.   Real
                                                              Make-Believe

4. A picnic blanket is on the grass.   Real
                                                              Make-Believe

5. A rabbit picks pears.   Real
                                                              Make-Believe

6. A little girl sees a lake.   Real
                                                              Make-Believe

7. A rabbit carries a bunch of   Real
    grapes.   Make-Believe

Macmillan/McGraw-Hill

7

Distinguish Between Fantasy and Reality

real

make-believe

Read each set of sentences. Underline the sentence that tells about something that is make-believe.

1. **a.** Sandy reads a book about dogs.

   b. The dog reads a book to Sandy.

   c. Sandy likes to read to her dog.

2. **a.** A rabbit can swim like a fish.

   b. A rabbit can eat greens.

   c. A rabbit can hop very fast.

3. **a.** Mom stopped the car at the red light.

   b. The light talked to the car.

   c. The car had four tires.

4. **a.** Nicole wrote a story about her cat.

   b. That story is about Nicole and her cat.

   c. The cat told a story about Nicole.

5. **a.** The seal drove a truck to the city.

   b. The seal rode in a truck to the city.

   c. Ben drove a truck filled with seals.

Macmillan/McGraw-Hill

5

Mr. Rabbit and the Lovely Present

 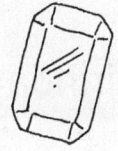 

Sapphires are blue like the sk**y**.

Read each sentence. Circle the word that completes each sentence. Then write the word.

1. The little girl began to _____.

   my
   shy
   cry

2. "_____ are you sad?" asked the rabbit.

   Why
   Pry
   Sly

3. "I can't afford to _____ a present," said the little girl.

   fry
   buy
   dry

4. "_____ your eyes," said the rabbit.

   Fly
   Why
   Dry

5. "We will _____ to think of a present for your mother."

   fry
   try
   sky

Phonogram *y*

My birthday is in Ju**ly**.

Circle the picture that goes with each word.

1. cry

2. dry

3. fly

4. shy

5. buy

SOUND/LETTER RELATIONSHIPS:
Long Vowels and Phonograms (/ī/-*y*)

Level 5 MR. RABBIT AND THE LOVELY PRESENT

5

Macmillan/McGraw-Hill

Mr. Rabbit and the Lovely Present

Often you can use the meaning of words you do know to figure out the meaning of an unfamiliar word.

Read each sentence. Use other words in the sentence to help you figure out the meaning of the underlined word. Fill in the circle next to the meaning of the word.

1. The little girl could not **afford** to buy her mother emeralds.
   - ○ having enough time to do something
   - ○ having a wish to do something
   - ○ having enough money to do something

2. The rabbit thought the mother would like a red **fire engine**.
   - ○ truck used to fight fires
   - ○ an engine that causes fires
   - ○ a person who fights fires

3. The girl often ate green **spinach** for dinner.
   - ○ a green mat used at the dinner table
   - ○ a green leafy vegetable
   - ○ a kind of green caterpillar

Unfamiliar Words

A _____ can fly.
It lives in a tree.

cat   bird

Read each story. Use the words you know to figure out the missing word. Then circle the word.

1. Your _____ are for seeing.
   You have two of them on
   your face. Your nose
   is under them.

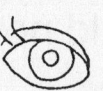

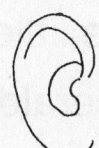

   eyes   ears

2. The little boy will _____ in his
   bed all night. He will wake up
   in the morning.

   play   sleep

3. Jack likes to _____ books.
   He enjoys books about
   monsters.

   ride   read

4. A _____ has a shell for a home.
   It likes to hide in the shell.
   It moves very slowly.

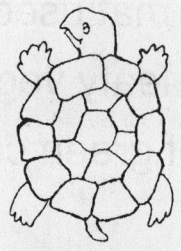

   turtle   rabbit

Macmillan/McGraw-Hill

4

Mr. Rabbit and the Lovely Present

The girl n**eed**s a birthday present for her mother.

Say each picture name. Listen to the beginning sound or sounds. Write the letter or letters that complete each word.

1.

fr   w

_____ **eed**

2.

sp   st

_____ **eed**

3.

f   tw

_____ **eed**

4.

n   s

_____ **eed**

5.

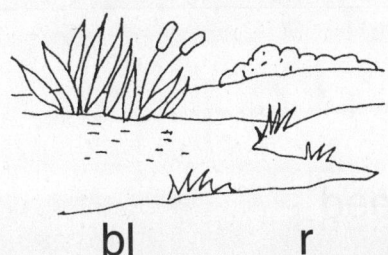

bl   r

_____ **eed**

6.

d   br

_____ **eed**

Phonogram *eed*

Ted will **feed** the birds.

Read each sentence. Circle the word that completes the sentence. Then write the word.

1.

feed   heed   need

Ted's mom will _____ help in the garden.

2.

breed   weed   heed

Ted will help pull the _____.

3.

seeds   reeds   weeds

Then he will plant some _____.

4.

need   speed   deed

Ted did his good _____ for the day.

4

Diphthong *ow*

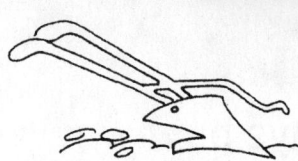

plow

Say each picture name. Circle and write the word that names the picture.

1.

now
bow
how

_____

2.

plow
brown
eyebrow

_____

3.

now
cow
wow

_____

4.

bow-wow
how now
meow

_____

4

Level 5 MR. RABBIT AND THE LOVELY PRESENT

Diphthong *ow*

A dog says **b**ow-**w**ow!

Read each riddle. Write the word from the box at the bottom of the page that answers each riddle.

1. This animal says moo. _____

2. An actor might do this at the end of a play. _____

3. You have one above each eye. _____

4. A farmer uses this in the fields. _____

5. It means right at this moment. _____

6. A cat says this. _____

| plow | meow | bow | now | cow | eyebrow |

Macmillan/McGraw-Hill

Name _____   Date _____

A Letter to Amy

Thinking about how a character feels can help you understand why the character does or says certain things in a story.

Read or reread "A Letter to Amy." Then write how you think Peter is feeling.

What Peter Is Doing	How Peter Feels
writing a letter to Amy	
thinking about what the boys will say when they see Amy at the party	
watching Amy run after the letter	
bumping into Amy	
waiting for Amy to come to his party	
blowing out the candles on his cake	

A Letter to Amy

Imagine that you are a friend of both Peter and Amy.
Write a letter to Amy to explain what happened when
Peter bumped into her. How could your letter help make
Amy feel better?

Dear Amy,

Peter told me about the mix-up. This is what really
happened. First Peter wrote you a letter

to _____

_____.

Next, when he went to mail the letter, _____

_____.

Then, he _____

_____.

Last, _____

_____.

Peter hopes you will still come to his party.

                              Your friend,

                    _____

Macmillan/McGraw-Hill

4

A Letter to Amy

Peter's letter blew d**own** the street.

_____

Read each sentence. Write a word from the box to finish each sentence.

town	down	brown	gown	clowns	crowns

1. Peter sat _____ to plan his party.

2. He did not want funny _____ .

3. He did not want gold or silver _____ .

4. He did want red and _____ balloons.

5. He walked to the party store in _____ .

6. The woman in a blue _____ sold him balloons.

Phonogram *own*

The clown has a fr**own**.

Look at each picture. Then read the question. Underline the word that answers the question. Then write the word.

1. Is the man wearing a crown or a gown?

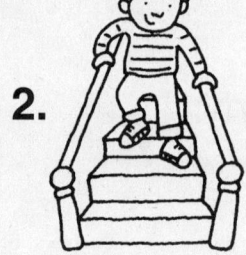

2. Is the boy going up or coming down?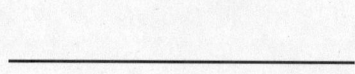

3. Is the woman wearing a gown or a frown?   _____

4. Is this person dressed as a crown or a clown?   _____

Macmillan/McGraw-Hill

Phonogram *out*

A Letter to Amy

The letter blew **out** of Peter's hand.

To is this Saturday at 2

Say each picture name. Circle and write the word that names the picture.

1.

pout
trout
stout

_____

2.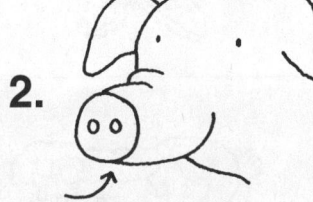

snout
scout
spout

_____

3.

stout
shout
sprout

_____

4.

snout
scout
spout

_____

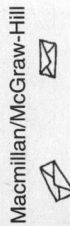

Macmillan/McGraw-Hill

Phonogram *out*

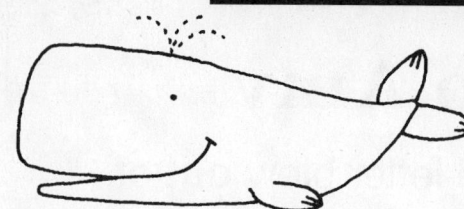

A whale can sp**out**.

Read each word. Circle the picture that goes with the word.

1. scout

2. trout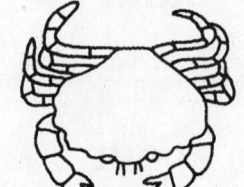

3. shout

4. pout

5. sprouts

Make, Confirm, or Revise Predictions

A Letter to Amy

Sometimes your predictions about what will happen in a story may be incorrect. This may happen because you did not understand a part of the story. Other times the author may not give enough clues.

Think about the predictions you made the first time you read "A Letter to Amy." Then fill in the answers in the chart below.

Question	Yes/No	Why or Why Not?
Did the story title help you make predictions?		
Were you surprised at what happened to the letter?		
Did you think Amy would see the letter before it was mailed?		
Did you think Amy would come to the party?		

Macmillan/McGraw-Hill

8

Level 5 A LETTER TO AMY

Make, Confirm, or Revise Predictions

Read each story. Then circle the answer to each question. Underline the clues in the story that helped you predict what will happen next.

1. Ezra came home at lunchtime. His head hurt. His stomach felt funny. His forehead was hot.
What will Ezra do next?
   a. go back to school
   b. stay home in bed
   c. go to a baseball game

2. Angela put on a robe. She had a funny red wig on her head. Then she walked onto the stage.
What will Angela do next?
   a. go to sleep
   b. go on a school trip
   c. act in a school play

3. Pedro takes his homework off the table. He helps his dad set the table. Then he calls his mom.
What will the family do next?
   a. eat dinner
   b. go to bed
   c. eat breakfast

4. Ling buys a bathing suit, a straw hat, and some shorts. When she gets home she packs a suitcase.
What will Ling do next?
   a. go to her office
   b. go to the post office
   c. take a trip

Name _____   Date _____

A Letter to Amy

In reading, you may see words that you do not know. Try using the words you do know to figure out the meanings of any new words. Then check the picture clues to see if you are correct.

Read each sentence. Circle the meaning of the underlined word. Use the other words and picture clues.

1. Peter saw a bright flash of lightning and heard the roar of **thunder**.

   a. loud noise of a strong wind
   b. loud noise that follows lightning
   c. loud sound of falling water

2. The letter blew across a **hopscotch** game marked on the sidewalk.

   a. hopping game played outside
   b. word game played with paper
   c. running game played with a ball

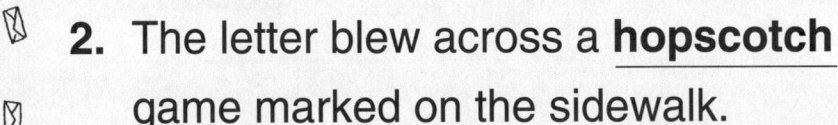

3. Peter stuffed the letter into a **mailbox**.

   a. a place to read your letters
   b. a place to put letters to be mailed
   c. a place to write your letters

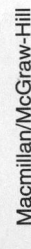

Unfamiliar Words

The _____ is a very tall person.
He can touch the top of a tree!

giant
father
farmer

Read each group of sentences. Use the words in the sentences to help you figure out the missing word. Then circle the word.

1. This plant is pretty when it _____.
   It will have many flowers.
   The flowers will be red.

   picks
   blooms
   rains

2. We put a _____ in that tree.
   A little bird lives there.
   It is her home.

   birdhouse
   robin
   aquarium

3. Ned _____ because he was sad.
   His eyes and nose got red.
   His face was all wet, too.

   jumped
   cried
   sang

4. The _____ comes up early in the morning.
   It goes down at night.
   In summer, it feels very hot.

   stars
   sun
   sky

Level 5 A LETTER TO AMY

Macmillan/McGraw-Hill

4

Phonogram *oil*

A car needs **oil** to run.

Say each picture name. Listen to the beginning sound or sounds. Write the letter or letters that complete each word.

1.

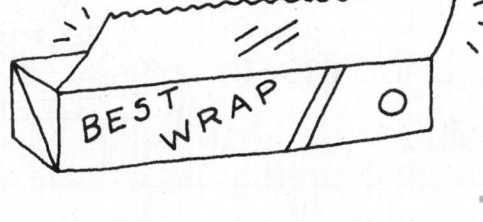

f   t

_____ **oil**

2.

c   b

_____ **oil**

3.

br   sp

_____ **oil**

4.

s   sp

_____ **oil**

5.

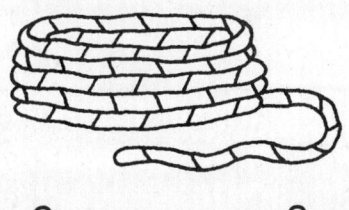

c   s

_____ **oil**

6.

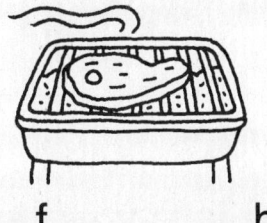

f   br

_____ **oil**

6

Learning the Code
SOUND/LETTER RELATIONSHIPS:
Diphthongs and Phonograms (/oi/-*oil*)

89

Phonogram *oil*

coil

Read each sentence. Circle the word that completes the sentence. Then write the word.

1.

Mom will _____ the meat.

broil   spoil   foil

2.

Roy put _____ in the car.

coil   toil   oil

3.

Jill put seeds in the _____.

soil   spoil   boil

4.

We put _____ around the pots.

boil   toil   foil

5.

The water will _____ in a minute.

oil   coil   boil

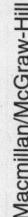

Use Alphabetical Order

A dictionary is a list of words with their meanings. These words are called entry words. The entry words are listed in ABC order. A definition explains the meaning of each entry word.

Use pages 274 and 275 in your book to answer these questions.

1. How many entry words are on page 275?

   _____

2. What entry word appears just before the entry word **black**? _____

3. Does the entry word **cereal** appear before or after the entry word **center**? _____

4. How many meanings can you find for the entry word **bite**? _____

5. Read the definition for **celebrate.** Write a sentence using the word **celebrate.**

   _____

Macmillan/McGraw-Hill

Use Alphabetical Order

You know that words in a dictionary are in ABC or alphabetical order. Use this guide to help you find the part of the dictionary you want.

FRONT	MIDDLE	BACK
Words Beginning with the Letters A–F	Words Beginning with the Letters G–P	Words Beginning with the Letters Q–Z

Read each word. Circle the part of the dictionary where you would find each word. Check your work with a dictionary.

1. apple   FRONT   MIDDLE   BACK

2. gas   FRONT   MIDDLE   BACK

3. queen   FRONT   MIDDLE   BACK

4. highway   FRONT   MIDDLE   BACK

5. bolt   FRONT   MIDDLE   BACK

6. tomato   FRONT   MIDDLE   BACK

7. mast   FRONT   MIDDLE   BACK

8. dawn   FRONT   MIDDLE   BACK

Macmillan/McGraw-Hill

Follow Directions

Sometimes directions tell you how to get from one place to another. Remember to follow the steps in the order in which they are written.

Study this map and read the directions. Then trace Myra's route from home to school on the map. Put a check in the box as you complete each step.

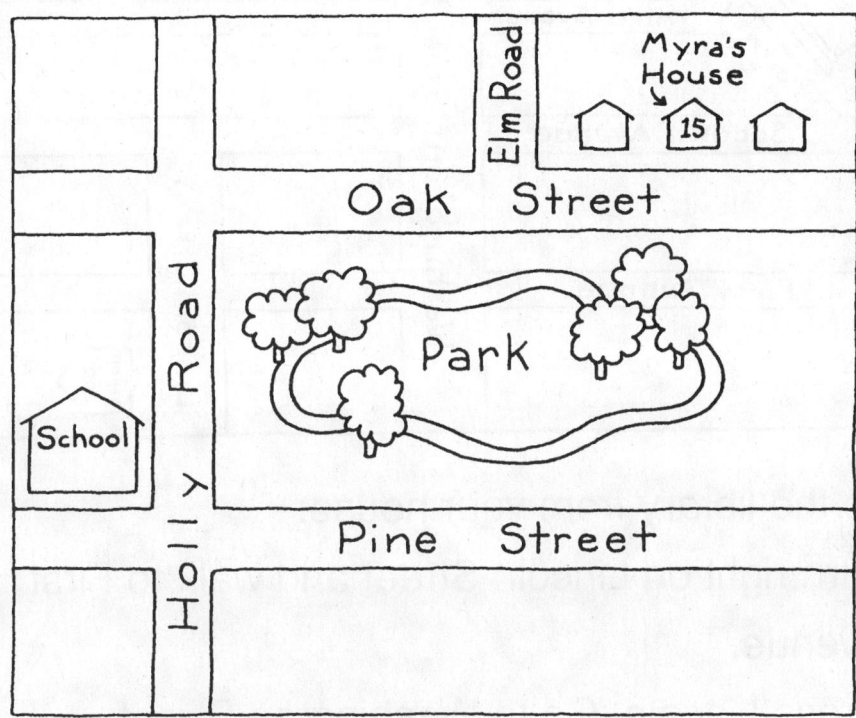

To get to school from Myra's house:

☐ **1.** Go out of the house to Oak Street.

☐ **2.** Turn right and walk to Elm Road.

☐ **3.** Cross Elm Road. Go to Holly Road.

☐ **4.** Cross Holly. Turn left. Cross Oak.

☐ **5.** Walk 1 block. The school is at the corner of Holly and Pine.

Follow Directions

Directions can help you get from one place to another. Imagine that you are new to town. A friend gives you this map and directions on how to get to the library. Read the directions. Then trace the route on the map. Check off each step as you complete it.

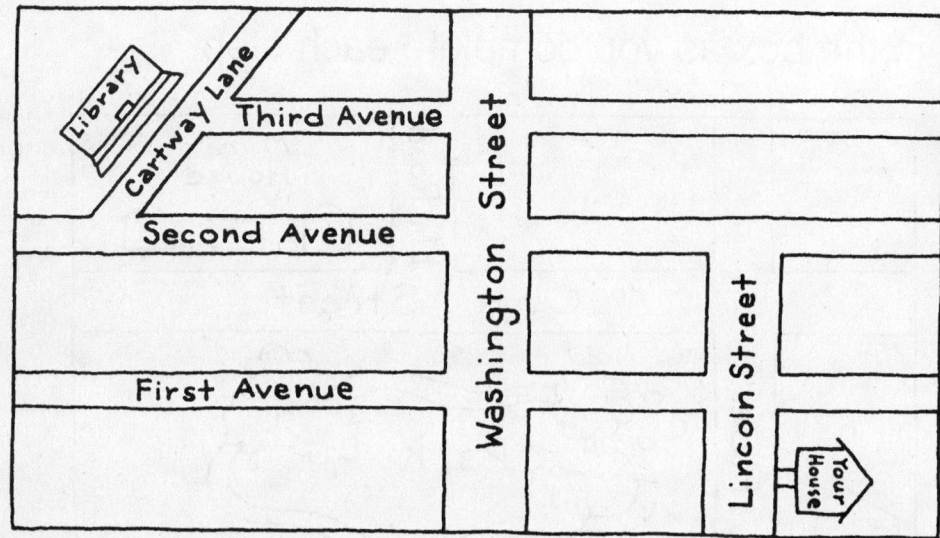

To get to the library from your house:

☐ **1.** Turn right on Lincoln Street and walk to First Avenue.

☐ **2.** Cross Lincoln. Go to Washington Street.

☐ **3.** Turn right. Cross First Avenue.

☐ **4.** Walk 1 block to Second Avenue.

☐ **5.** Cross Second Avenue and turn left. Cross Washington.

☐ **6.** Walk 1 block to Cartway Lane.

☐ **7.** Cross Cartway. Turn right and walk to the library.

7

My Notes

My Notes

My Notes

My Notes

My Notes

My Notes

My Notes

My Notes

My Notes

My Notes

My Notes

My Notes